TEILHARD DE CHARDIN
A NEW SYNTHESIS OF EVOLUTION

Teilhard de Chardin

A NEW SYNTHESIS OF EVOLUTION

JOSEPH V. KOPP

DEUS BOOKS
PAULIST PRESS
(Paulist Fathers)
Glen Rock, N. J.

Published by the Paulist Press
Editorial Office: 304 W. 58th St., N.Y 19. N.Y.
Business Office: Glen Rock, New Jersey
Originally published in German
by Rex-Verlag Luzern/Munchen
© The Mercier Press Ltd
1964
2nd Printing 1965
3nd Printing 1966
Nihil obstat: Edward J. Montano, S.T.D.
Censor Librorum
Imprimatur: Francis Cardinal Spellman
Archbishop of New York
January 17, 1964

Printed in the Netherlands 1964
by N.V. Drukkerij Bosch-Utrecht

Contents

Preface

A glance at the literature on Pierre Teilhard de Chardin which has been published up to now is enough to show that it will be some time before any sort of final judgment can be passed on his concepts of the world and mankind. It will take years before a complete scientific assessment can be made of the entire material available, and it is still uncertain what results it will produce.

In contrast we have the fact that Teilhard and his philosophy are already the theme of lively discussions, not only on the radio, in scientific papers, discussion groups and lectures to cultural societies, but even in the popular press. One may consider it to be premature, but the fact remains that Teilhard is a subject for discussion all over the world and will continue to attract attention in ever wider circles.

That innumerable people, therefore, especially those of Christian belief, are following these discussions with intense interest, is understandable and, since they are concerned with questions of the greatest religious importance, extremely gratifying.

However, these discussions on the radio and in the press can only be followed by those who are sufficiently familiar with the scientist's theories. Although this knowledge is best obtained from the published works of Pierre Teilhard himself, it is not easy for everyone to gather his information in this way, owing to the quan-

tity and the, to some extent, completely new phraseology of Teilhard's writings.

Up to now a description of the scientist, his philosophy and his place in the history of evolutionary thought in short, simple terms for the uninitiated, has been lacking. It is this need, and this need only, that the following pages set out to fill.

It has been necessary at times to clarify the often somewhat vague and diffuse expressions used by Teilhard and to emphasize certain ideas. Only thus is it possible to avoid the emasculation of his philosophy, for which many of his adherents are striving, in order to save the scientist's work from rejection by a wide circle. The reader of these pages should always bear in mind how very sharp the contrast often is between Teilhard's theories and those still generally accepted.

There is another, more delicate point: those familiar with Teilhard's works are agreed that the extraordinarily powerful effect that his philosophy has on the modern reader cannot be accounted for only by the contents of his works. Very powerful elements in its presentation also come into play: the intrepid determination of his views, the sheer poetic strength of his prose and, above all, his unusual way of rising imperceptibly from strict scientific judgment into intuitive thought. This mastery over the physical medium of communicating his conviction is partly why, for most readers, his writings represent not only the acquisition of new knowledge but also a deep spiritual experience. This can be verified by means of a small experiment: if one takes from his philosophy only the facts capable of strict, scientific proof and ignores every excursion into the realm of intuition, the real Teilhard de Chardin is no longer there. That the strength as well as the weakness of his work is to be found in this method of thought and presentation is obvious.

For this reason, to judge Teilhard de Chardin fairly, one must decide — and it is by no means easy — whether or not to accept this predicative dimension that is peculiar to him. The author regards this acceptance as only right and proper. Teilhard's scientific and intuitive beliefs should not be set out in pre-digested form. Even when they are abridged, the reader should feel something of the almost magical influence exercised by his concepts, in which it is impossible to separate the scientific from the intuitive-prophetic without damaging the whole. Finally an author can claim the right that even a simplified exposition of his ideas should not be deprived of the method by which he himself has conveyed his convictions. The choice of this manner of representation may be seen as a sign of reverence for the scientist's world of ideas.

This work then tries to describe Teilhard de Chardin's person and philosophy, and to distinguish his ideas from those that preceded his. That is all. Critical discussion has been avoided because the time is not yet ripe, and because to attempt it in so short a work would be indefensible. The reader's attention will only be drawn now and then to the problems that will confront Christian teaching should Teilhard's concepts be proved right.

In the meantime it must be admitted that numerous discussions over Teilhard de Chardin give rise to the fear that, in some places, much may be rejected sim-

ply because it is new and inconvenient. This fear is all the more reason for a sympathetic and careful examination of the ideas he presents.

I The Lost Lawsuit

At the start of the 18th century natural science was still unquestionably influenced by the biblical account of the creation. Hardly anyone doubted that the various types of plants, animals, and humans were all brought into being from the start by successive but unrepeated acts of creation by God. According to the evidence of biblical genealogy, the age of the earth was reckoned to be nine thousand years at the most. Fossils discovered here and there were explained as tricks of nature or remnants of the Flood. And that was that.

The first doubts to be cast on the traditional conception of the creation were counter to this biblical calculation of the earth's age. The Chinese put it at several million years, and the Jesuits at the Imperial Court in Peking brought their ideas to Europe. As early as 1747 the French biologist, Buffon, put the earth's age at seventy-five thousand years, and that of the first living organisms at thirty-five thousand. Fossils too were gradually being recognized as the remains of early plants and animals. In 1809, the biologist Lamarck published his theory of evolution according to which all living creatures were continually developing their structure to suit surrounding conditions. In his opinion the minute changes thus achieved were passed on to the next generation and in the course of thousands of years resulted in completely new forms of life. Lamarck's theory has been disproved, however, since the study of heredity shows that acquired characteristics are not hereditary. But the basic idea of a continuous development was correct. In 1831 the English geologist, Charles Lyell, calculated the age of sedimentary rock to be two hundred and fifty million years.

In the same year, 1831, Charles Darwin, a 22-year-old theological student passionately interested in biology, was offered an active part in the voyage around the world of the "Beagle." He took Lyell's book with him. He had six years in which to reflect on the problem of the earth's development, and during this time also had the opportunity to observe a vast number of strange biological forms. On his return, Darwin, already a disciple of the evolutionary theory, made an intensive study of the results of English animal breeding. Finally, in 1859, at a time when evolutionary thinking was very much in the air, he acceded to the requests of his friends and published his classic work *The Origin of Species*.

Darwin's explanation of evolution as resulting solely from natural selection and the battle for existence was incomplete since the mutation factor was not yet known, but his basic theory that life on our planet had developed from a single source was correct.

Opinions on Darwin's work were divided. Great scientists greeted the new concept with enthusiasm and gave Darwin courage to pursue his chosen path despite opposition. Others, among them friends, rejected it. Here too, as in every walk of life, jealousy played a part.

Darwin himself combined modesty with scholarship.

He carefully avoided all polemics and only hinted, with the greatest caution, that the human race was no exception in the development of life. Above all he was anxious to hurt nobody's religious feelings. In fact one could almost say Darwin was not a "Darwinian."

Unfortunately certain schools of thought then presented Darwin's discovery from the wrong angle. In the very same year, 1859, Friedrich Engels wrote to Karl Marx: "Incidentally Darwin, whom I am just reading, is absolutely splendid. One bastion of theology was still unbreached. Now it has fallen."

Karl Marx replied a month later: "I have read Darwin's book during the last four weeks. Although set out in the clumsy English style, this is the book that will provide the natural history basis for our work." This unjustified appropriation of the evolutionary theory by the Materialists was only *one* of many unfortunate incidents.

On the Christian side, the battle was taken up personally by the Anglican Bishop of Oxford, Samuel Wilberforce. This dignitary appeared with a warlike band of followers, including a number of pious women, at an historic meeting of the British Association at Oxford on June 30, 1860. He conducted the attack against Darwin with a brilliance of rhetoric quite unhampered by any knowledge of the facts. Neither could this prince of the Church resist the temptation of making fun of the matter and inquiring after his opponent's simian ancestors. The meeting broke up in tumult and hostility.

Such was the unfortunate debut of one of the greatest and most vital discoveries in the history of mankind.

In the hundred years that have passed since then scientific methods have continually improved. The earth's crust, too, has provided one proof after another from its archives. Above all, the discovery of what are called mutations (immediate transformations of hereditary material) has joined forces with the Darwinian theories of the battle for existence and natural selection to produce a decisive result. Evolution, including that of the human race, is today an almost established fact. Only the scientifically inexplicable driving force remains unresolved, in other words, the *how* of evolution.

The Materialists, as we have seen, enthusiastically adopted the concept of evolution, developed it on purely mechanistic lines, and made it the basis of their whole interpretation of the universe. In their opinion, everything that exists, including the human intellect, is material which is in conflict with itself and thus evolves. This, it is true, presents a somewhat sinister picture, but it is one of monumental coherence.

In this new situation, the behavior of Christians of all denominations was not very sensible. True, the Church itself had never publicly disputed the theory of evolution, but Christian circles felt Darwin's teaching to be an attack on the very heart of their philosophy. Unfortunately, they felt themselves obliged to defend not only the *theological* content of the Mosaic account of creation: that a spiritual, personal God, outside this world, had called the whole of creation into being out of nothing. They also fought, disastrously, for the *original, static theory of life,* in which the ingenious author of the Book of Genesis had wrapped up his theological statements: God had, in several separate acts of creation, called all living things into being, complete and enduring, as we see them today. Added to this, these circles believed that the Christian concept of man as the unique, transcendental, spiritual and immortal image of God was threatened by the evolutionary concept of creation.

Subjectively this conflict was very understandable at first. Fossil evidence was still very scarce and the evolutionary explanation of the creation therefore still no more than a hypothesis. The opposition was also psychologically forgivable since the theory of evolution, viewed, superficially, appeared to support the purely materialistic-mechanistic view of the world. But *objectively* this conflict was a disaster for Christianity, since it opposed not only the materalistic interpretation, but also the theory of development which had been proved correct a thousand times over. This is why literature of defense against Darwin reads today like the papers of a lost lawsuit.

The more "documents" the earth's crust released, the more untenable became the position of this opposition which had been wrong from the start. The defensive attitude of the Church party finally led to the false position where each new fossil discovered was hailed as another proof of the materialistic philosophy and another argument against the Christian concept of creation. This was what gave rise to the regrettable distrust between religious circles and modern scientists which, even today, has by no means been overcome.

Under the weight of the evidence, concessions were gradually made and the theory of evolution was widely accepted, but as far as the origin of life, above all, human life, was concerned, it was held that God had intervened exceptionally in His own work. But such special intervention made the scientists uneasy, and in the end Christian biologists and theologians agreed on the formula of separate jurisdiction. Religion and science were to study the same phenomena from completely different angles. Biology was to remain "material" – in other words, to confine itself strictly to matter and its properties, and was authorized to make statements about the human body only. Statements about man as a spiritual phenomenon were reserved to philosophy and theology. It was rather like sticking in little flags to mark armistice positions on a map. For a time the magic formula of separate jurisdiction did bring about a certain kind of peace, but on closer inspection it was soon recognized as an escape. The decisive point in question lay in No-man's-land. Both sides now abandoned it. In this situation two half answers did not add up to a whole. There can be no real discussion in this sort of situation where the two parties are separated by a door without a handle.

This is still the situation today.

Although the Encyclical *Humani generis* (1950) leaves the question of the physical origin of mankind to science, this only served to confirm the existing state of affairs and did not solve the problem. In reality the Church presents no interpretation of the traditional expressions "Our First Parents," "The Garden of Eden," "The Fall," "Original Sin," that would allow a present-day Christian to interpret the scientifically proven facts of the origin of man in a manner that would be even vaguely theologically acceptable. This is a serious handicap for any honest seeker after truth. The yeast is there but it may not be mixed with the dough.

When one thinks how completely human thought has gone over to the side of science during the last decade, when one considers that scientific discoveries have increased at such a rate that in the last twenty years we have gained a deeper insight into the structure of matter and life than was gained during the previous thousand, one realizes how rapidly the intellectual position has worsened for a Christian who comes into contact – indeed whose conscience *forces* him to come into contact – with new scientific discoveries, if acceptable theological explanations of the results of modern experiments are not soon forthcoming.

One symptom of the need felt by countless honest seekers of knowledge is that the works of the late scientist Pierre Teilhard de Chardin whose books have recently been published, have already sold millions of copies.

This introduction to the present state of affairs is essential if we are to pass judgment on Pierre Teilhard de Chardin and his works. Only against this background can the urgency of his message and the true depths of his philosophy be fully appreciated.

II The Nomad of Science

At this point it might be advantageous to review the scientist's life, for in it we find that coincidence of being and thinking which has always been the hallmark of truly great minds. The credibility of his interpretation of the universe is based in some measure on his stature as a scientist.

Pierre Teilhard de Chardin was born May 1st, 1881 in the little village of Orcines near Clermont Ferrand. He was the fourth of eleven children in a family of Auvergne squirearchy. He and his brothers and sisters were taught by their father about the stones, plants and animals of the *Massif Central*. When only six, Pierre had already started a collection in a secret corner of the house – iron and other bits of metal – especially shell-fragments from the nearby training area. To the child, iron appeared harder, heavier and more absolutely perfect than anything he knew. Iron possessed the highest quality of all – permanency. This was the first impression matter made on his youthful mind. But one day it had been raining, and the young collector discovered with horror that his pieces of iron were covered with rust. So iron was not permanent after all! Then he started a collection of stones of different colors and shapes, stones with which he was to occupy himself for the rest of his life.

Later Pierre Teilhard followed family tradition by becoming a pupil at the Jesuit College of Notre Dame de Mongré, near Lyons. His school friends remember him as a lonely, solitary boy. He was generally at the top of his class except in religion. Apparently the way in which God was referred to seemed to worry him.

In 1899 he entered the Society of Jesus at Aix en Provence. When the Jesuits were banished from France in 1904 he continued studying philosophy and theology on the Channel Island of Jersey. Although already deeply interested in the connection between theology and the phenomena of cosmic life, he continued to study petrology and never went for a walk without a geological hammer and a magnifying glass. The Anglo-Norman island proved fruitful ground for his first experiments.

From 1905 to 1908 we find Teilhard teaching physics and chemistry at Ismailia, in Egypt. This time spent in the East was to have a lasting influence on his love for the earth. It was here that he first realized the meaning of evolution, that the whole world is in a continuous, irresistible state of becoming, rising from a previous "Less" to an ever more refined "More."

About this time (1905) Henri Bergson's work *Creative Evolution* was published, casting doubt on a purely rational science and seeking to find a connection between mind and matter. It recognized the existence of unknown powers and strove after a deeper explanation for the origin of life than that provided by extreme mechanistic Darwinism. Pierre Teilhard devoured the book. The idea of a creative *élan vital* made a deep impression on the young scholar and destroyed forever his conception of an unchanging world.

From 1908 to 1912 he was in Sussex where he

worked with leading scientists studying, chiefly, fossil life in rocks, quarries and clay deposits. Just before his ordination at Hastings in 1911 he made the unusual resolution, difficult for the uninitiated to understand, to devote his life to the study of fossils. It was then that he had his first serious differences with the traditionally dualistic attitudes to mind and matter, soul and body, the conscious and the unconscious, and his conviction grew that mind and matter are not two antagonistic substances but two conditions, two aspects of the same cosmic stuff.

In 1912 Pierre Teilhard returned to France and worked at the laboratory of the *Musée d'Histoire naturelle* in Paris under the distinguished paleontologist, Marcellin Boule.

During World War I he served as a corporal in the medical corps. He was in battle after battle on the Aisne, the Somme and at Verdun. His comrades praised his courage and self-sacrifice, and he was decorated with the Legion of Honor. Here, in this melting pot, where millions of men were existing under increased psychological pressure, he first realized the magnitude of man. For him war became a scientific experiment. In the midst of battle he felt humanity to be a super-individual phenomenon, a biological entity rising above the individual, as the Noósphere.*

In 1919 at the age of 38 he was appointed Profes-

---

* A word coined by Teilhard de Chardin to denote the layer of life with the power of reflective thought (Gr. noos) which covers the world. *Biosphere* is the layer below that, of life without reflective thought. Crouched in the trenches he jotted down these and similar ideas on odd scraps of paper.

sor of Geology at the *Institut Catholique* in Paris. His superiors, still imbued with the static theory of life, did not know Teilhard and expected the young scholar to smash Darwin's theories. He was to do this but not in the way they had expected. But he soon encountered difficulties in his teaching and a trivial incident led to a decisive turning point. A young theologian visited him to discuss the conflict between faith and knowledge. Pierre Teilhard noted down for him, on a couple of closely written pages, his views on original sin. These pages were read by too many and, worse still, by unauthorized persons. The result was that envy and ill will, came to the surface. His superiors found it advisable to remove the young professor from Paris. A providential decision!

In 1923 Teilhard was invited by his fellow Jesuit, the geologist Licent, to join an expedition to Eastern Mongolia, sponsored and financed by the National Museum. This was the start of what he called the "Asian Adventure." In 1924, accompanied by crates of fossils, he returned to Paris to his professorial chair and to the laboratories of the *Musée d'Histoire naturelle*. But by 1926 he was off again to the East. He joined in numerous expeditions with Fr. Licent, partly for the Chinese Government's Geological Service, and partly at the request of other governments, institutes and private companies. He became a nomad of science. Although a great deal of his life was spent in laboratories, he remained an out-door savant, always ready to start out anew, in the grip of an irresistible wanderlust, a restless urge to plunge into what he called the "ocean of matter."

21

The years 1926–27 found him in Mongolia and on the Yellow River. At the request of Chinese, American and Swedish scholars he was given charge of the fossil excavations in East Asia. This, in turn, brought more financial aid for his work. In 1928 he was on the Red Sea, in French Somaliland and Abyssinia.

In December 1928 a team of young Chinese trained entirely by Pierre Teilhard discovered the skull of the "Pekin Man," *Sinanthropus Pekinensis,* at Chow-Kow-Tien, about thirty miles from Peking. It was one of the most important paleontological events of the twentieth century. As a result, Teilhard became scientific advisor to the official Geological Survey Service of China. This led to other expeditions, chiefly in Manchuria, up to the Siberian border, and in the Gobi desert. The Croisière Jaune Crusade from Peking to Turkestan, financed by Citroën, the French automobile company, in which he took part as geological expert, lasted from April 1931 to February 1932.

At the beginning of 1933 he traveled around North America and lectured at universities and institutions in New York and Chicago. A journey to Honolulu and Japan followed. After that he returned to Paris for a time, then went back to Peking and finally to Washington where he lectured on fossilized human remains in China at the Pan-Pacific Geological Congress. After a tour through North America he returned to Peking.

With the courage and endurance of the true pioneer, Teilhard de Chardin was always ready to start off on the track of prehistoric man at every fresh clue. He traveled for months in mule caravans, on horseback, in two-wheeled wagons and in trucks to the farthest corners of the earth and often through unexplored territory far from civilization, exposed to freezing cold, burning heat, sandstorms and every conceivable natural calamity, to say nothing of marauding bands. No detail escaped his experienced eye. Anything he found of note pertaining to geology, geography, topography, paleontology, zoology, botany and ethnography was noted and assimilated. Not the least of his interests were the racial characteristics, mentality, way of life and habit of thought of the countless tribes among whom he lived. A thousand paths and a thousand thoughts but only one idea: to get on the track of the secret of the earth, to find the yardstick to measure man so that the rightful place of this puzzling being in the scheme of nature could be found.

All this time he was, of course, publishing the results of his experiments in zoology and paleontology in various scientific periodicals all over the world. Since 1934 more and more of his writings and treatises on the theological interpretation of man and evolution had been circulating among the French intellectual élite. Generally handwritten, they were passed from one person to another giving fresh strength to innumerable searches after truth.

In 1935 there was an expedition to Northern India and Java and the years from 1936–39 were also dedicated to continuous work on the earth's crust. We find World Citizen Teilhard in Philadelphia, New York, Paris, in China, on expeditions to Burma and Java, in Japan and finally back in China.

At the outbreak of the Second World War in 1939 he was interned in Peking. During his enforced stay he wrote his key work *Le Phénomène Humain*.* In 1946 he returned to Paris and spent six years in a bare cell of his Order near the *Invalides*. He was in his sixties. Around him gathered all the restless, unsatisfied intellectuals: students, scholars, geologists, Christians and atheists, among the latter principally Marxists dissatisfied with their creed of a purely materialistic world. His days were filled with meetings, talks and private discussions.

In 1948 he submitted *Le Phénomène Humain* for censorship in Rome. It was turned down. But it was circulated privately among many thousands of readers, especially young French clerics. In 1950 the French *Académie des Sciences* elected him as a member.

Church circles had no doubts as to his genius or his faith. But Father Teilhard was not diplomatic enough, he was an *enfant terrible*. Once again he was considered unsuitable for Paris and in 1951 at the age of 70 he went into his final exile. In justice to his superiors it must be said that they always let their embarrassing son choose a place where he could best continue his scientific work.

This time Teilhard de Chardin was summoned to the Wenner-Gren Foundation for Anthropological Research in New York. From there he traveled all over North and South America to whatever places were the centers of scientific experiments at the moment. In 1951 and 1953 the old scholar once more joined expeditions to South Africa where, in his opinion, the human race originated. In the spring of 1954 he went to Paris for

* Published in English as *The Phenomenon of Man*, Collins, 1959.

24

the last time and gave a purely scientific lecture about South Africa. Once more pettiness and jealousy were aroused. Teilhard – stumbling block and symbol of controversy – cut short his stay and fled to his laboratory in New York.

On Easter Sunday evening. April 10, 1955, the 74-year-old wanderer had a stroke in the middle of an animated discussion and collapsed. A month earlier, at a reception in the French Consulate, he had said he would like to die on the Feast of the Resurrection.

That is but a brief outline of the scientist's life. His unceasing query had been: "Where does man come from? Where does he go to? What is man's place and meaning within the cosmos?"

To Bring Together What Has Become Separated

Naturally there were other Christians, both priests and laymen, affected by these arguments over the meaning of the biblical account of creation. The contradictory answers given by scientists disturbed innumerable people and drew them into the conflict. But few were so deeply affected by this divergence of opinions as Pierre Teilhard. Most of them studied this delicate subject for a time, sensed the contradictions and returned to their daily occupations. Their hearts were not broken. They simply added these questions to the other unsolved problems of this world and continued their everyday lives.

But not Father Teilhard. He celebrated Mass daily,

read his breviary, carried out his spiritual exercises and passed the rest of his time in laboratories and on expeditions. He was tireless in his pursuit of prehistoric and early man. Scientist and Christian! His days were spent in the borderland where biblical and scientific concepts meet and clash. Not for one moment did he leave this danger zone. The vast quantity of fossil evidence, and his conviction of man's unique position in the realm of life, drove him ceaselessly in the search for a greater, deeper meaning to evolution. The divergence of concepts finally became his ruling obsession.

He lived his whole life torn between two opposite poles. On the one side his conviction of the supernatural greatness and destiny of man in the cosmos, on the other his scientific conscience which forbade him to ignore even one paleontological discovery. Pierre Teilhard had never possessed that happy ability, common to so many, of being able to live in a world at cross-purposes with the faith they cherish in their hearts.

Man in the Bible and the man he dug up in a cave somewhere in China out of a 100,000-year-old deposit were one and the same man for him. He *could* not separate the personal God of Israel and that which he felt cosmically to be Point Alpha of the Universe. The meaning for him of intellectual and spiritual life was the finding of a solution to this problem. This inability to live in uncertainty was the cause and motivation of all his intellectual striving after a new cosmic concept.

His unceasing search in all corners of the earth, his continual vital, personal contact with the widest variety of peoples, races, creeds and cultures, the constant descents into the deep strata of prehistoric man and the brilliant intellectual discussions with the most learned scientists in the world, provided him not only with the intellectual but also with the intensely spiritual knowledge of the mysterious phenomenon, man, a knowledge which made the finding of a comprehensive interpretation of him an ever more urgent task.

We find his opinions on the world and mankind set down chiefly in his key work *Le Phénomène Humain*. The title itself tells us that the author did not intend to write a philosophical or theological treatise. As a *scientist* he examines man as he *appears* within the cosmos. His book is intended only to be an introduction to an explanation of the world and mankind and to some extent to provide philosophers and theologians with a basis to work on. But Pierre Teilhard takes the whole manifestation of man as the object of his research, the "within" as well as the "without." In his opinion man belongs in his *entirety* to nature. The *whole* of man is a product of our earth. He is, therefore, in his entirety, subject to the demands and methods of science. Anthropology is only really anthropology when it deals with man as a whole. That is why Pierre Teilhard as a scientist wants to collect every facet of man known to modern science into a coherent picture and then interpret it.

III   The "Within" of Cosmic Matter

The scientist first turned his attention to the stage before life, in other words to the *material* of which the world is made up. Let us take a glance at his thought on this subject.

Physicists used to regard the world as being composed of a system of unchangeable elements maintaining each other in equilibrium. Today we know this static conception of the world to be false. Just as in a photograph a firework exploding appears static whereas in reality every single spark is in a state of movement and transformation, so it is with creation. The world appears static only to our momentary view of it. In reality what we see of the cosmos is only a paper-thin cross section of a tree whose roots reach down to the unfathomed depths of the past, and whose branches rise to the unimaginable heights of the future. The whole world was, is and always will be a continually changing mass. Everything in the world originated from an arrangement of a few elements and transforms itself according to a law of increasing complexification. The material of the world has a propensity driving it from the simple to the complex. It has an "inherent preference," a natural tendency toward the complex. Cosmic matter concentrates itself into increasingly highly organized material forms.

This cosmic phenomenon must be explained. According to Teilhard there is only *one* sufficient, logical explanation. He calls it the "within" of things.

The scientist made the following reflections: some cosmic phenomena become visible, measurable or capable of scientific confirmation only when they have reached a certain degree of intensity. For instance, we can verify the fact that speed exercised a fundamental influence on the mass of a body only through use of the exceptionally high speeds reached by accelerated particles. Yet mass is altered by any speed, however slight. But, these alterations are immeasurable by man. Another example: chemical elements appear unchangeable, but the discovery of radioactivity proves this to be an illusion. Thus every body gives out some radiation, but we cannot measure any except those that we call radioactive material. However, it is wrong to conclude that what we cannot measure does not exist.

It is much the same with what Pierre Teilhard calls the "within" or "consciousness" of matter. In man, who stands at the summit of creation, the evidence of a "within" or "consciousness" is immediately obvious and undisputed. Neither can we dispense with this "within" when considering the behavior of the vertebrates. Even the conduct of insects and coelenterates cannot be explained without a "within." But we find this "within" less easy to grasp as soon as we move on to the plant world. The farther we go down the scale, the more difficult it becomes to establish the existence of this "within."

Bacteriologists and, still more, physicists and chemists, only deal with the "without" of their subjects because, due to its low intensity, the "within" is no longer significant. This is why science confined the phenomenon of consciousness to the higher forms of life. But this is a fallacy. The "within" or "consciousness" is a dimension that informs all cosmic matter, albeit at different intensities. The whole physical world contains a psyche but in differing concentrations. Just as man's body goes back to the first atom, so his spirit goes back just as far, only this cannot be demonstrated experimentally.

Thus we see that original matter is more than the multitude of atoms that modern science has so wonderfully analyzed. Even at the lowest, apparently purely mechanical, level a form of consciousness is concealed, admittedly extremely slight, but indispensable thereafter for an explanation of cosmic evolution. We have no right, therefore, to limit the origin of this "within" or "consciousness" to where we can first prove it. For the concept to be coherent, life inevitably demands a stage previous to life: the "within" of inanimate material. Thus in the whole cosmos, the material externals, which is all that science generally deals with, are accompanied by a usually concealed conscious spirit.

In so-called inanimate matter, this "conscious within" is not a coherent structure, but similarly composed to the matter itself. The "without," like the "within," is still atomic or granular. The fact that scientists believe the first living entities to have been a kind of large molecule in size and number, permits this inference. In the course of time the elements of the "conscious" become more complicated and refined just as the elements of exterior matter do. So the "conscious" is a cosmic property of varying intensity, the course of which we can follow through all the stages of life's growth, right up to man's reflective thinking. In a way the "conscious" resembles a spectrum: in man at the top of the scale we see it bright and unmistakable. Thereafter the colors blend into each other until at the bottom of the scale the darker colors are lost in obscurity.

The increasingly highly developed "conscious" is always accompanied outwardly by a correspondingly better and more complete material framework. Its complexity increases in geometrical progression. This phenomenon is an everyday affair and appears in millions of different guises. Spiritual perfection and material complexity are thus two facets of one and the same manifestation. The entire universe must therefore be regarded as a transition. Its foundations are formed of a few very simple elements with a poor "within": they are the subject of physics and chemistry and can be mathematically expressed. Going up the scale leads to a large number of very complex combinations with much richer "withins." They belong to biology and can no longer be mathematically expressed.

According to Teilhard de Chardin nothing can suddenly come to light after various stages of evolution which was not in some form present, even if unknown, from the beginning. In a lesser form everything in the world, including man, has existed since the beginning of time. That is cosmic embryogenesis. At a given moment the birth of a complete entity in time follows.

As we have seen, according to Pierre Teilhard an intrinsic part of the "within" of cosmic matter is a force that drives the universe toward an ever more complex and centralized state. The cosmos is rising in a spiral toward an ever denser inwardness.

It may be noted in passing that Teilhard de Chardin conjectured the existence of similar conditions in the rest of the cosmos, but confined his research to our planet since, at the moment, it is the only part of the universe where it is possible for us to trace evolution through to its final phases.

THE DEVELOPMENT OF LIFE

The scientist then turned his attention to the origin of life. In his opinion we will never know exactly how the organic developed from the chemical, the living from the not-yet-living, since the matter involved in the transition was so delicate that it has dissolved in strata long-since transformed. The secret lies forever with God. The riddle could be partly solved only if science succeeds in repeating the process in the laboratory. In any case, the origin of life is not, according to Teilhard de Chardin, a simple, steady progress. With the appearance of life a door was opened. The cell was the start of a new order developing from a crisis of the first importance.

For our scientist this emergence of life from the long period of the megamolecular zone of "sublife" consisted in an increase of the synthetic character of matter, in an advance to a higher degree of complexity. And this higher external complexity is always accompanied by a higher grade of "consciousness" or "interiority." So life is not the start of the psychic, but only a sudden upward metamorphosis of it. Life is the explosion of "interior energy" under biological high tension into the next stage of development.

Now comes the important problem of the *development of the organism*. For Pierre Teilhard, the struggle for existence, natural selection and the sudden appearance of mutations are realities, but they cannot explain the higher development of life. As we have said, in his view there is a force in the center of matter which systematically makes life more complex. This development of life is accomplished with a certain unanimity. In his eyes the entire biosphere, the living integument enveloping the earth, is one gigantic organism. Within it there is a systematic reaching upward. All living things seek for the highest and latest development. The biosphere resembles a forest of groping tendrils. If one of these tendrils finds a favorable mutation, that is, an opening promising access to a new plane of life, then, instead of continuing a homogenous existence, it gains a fresh mobility. It starts on a fresh line of development. The pulse of life renews itself on this newly found path. From this new shoot a second emerges, and then a third, and so on, always provided the new path is a good one. This is the origin of the *one* great tree of life from which all living things spring like branches.

Counter to this view of Pierre Teilhard is the argument that life on this earth does not appear to us today to derive from a single stem in the first place. Plants and animals appear as separate from each other as islands in the sea. We see a great many single trees growing without any connection to each other. Teilhard declares this retrospective view to be an optical illusion. In his opinion it is only now that the isolated groups appear as individual trees. In reality they are what remains of branches that once sprang one after another from the tree of life. Many extinct intermediary stages will be discovered, while others, despite the zeal of paleontologists, will remain unknown forever.

A further objection is that no transitional forms have ever been found in the natural archives of the earth. Paleontology has discovered only completed forms. The first mammal, no matter how primitive, was a mammal. The first of the *equidae,* was a horse. Opposing this view, Father Teilhard refers to the law of the extinction of sources.* All first attempts are delicate and fleeting. A young zoological group is not yet consolidated. The first stages are always weak and therefore liable to destruction. It is not only here that time wipes out first traces. Where is the first Greek? Where is the first Roman? Where is the first carriage? Where is the first weaver's shuttle? The first biological trial phases were incapable of fossilization, they were too soft and frail. It is moreover probable that we only find organisms as fossils when they are large enough, when their forms had become stabilized and they existed in large quantities. This is why we only find consolidated forms in the archives of the earth's crust.

So according to Teilhard de Chardin, evolution possesses a definite direction, progressing on a chosen axis. It appears as a clear line of progress. From one

* "Suppression of peduercles" is the term used in *The Phenomenon of Man.*

zoological stratum to another we find development, or sudden transition, continually pressing forward in the same direction. And in this upward development there are two common features that act as yardsticks of progress: the nervous system, which becomes notably more refined and concentrated in the transitions from stratum to stratum, and the brain which becomes larger and more convoluted. These are the external proofs of evolution's determination to achieve its goal. But, since nerves and brain are only features and dimensions of the conscious, this only proves once more that evolution, seen from within, is a development of the "spiritual." We must conclude, therefore, that evolution is primarily of a psychic nature.

Accordingly, biogenesis (ramification of life) is in the first place psychogenesis (ramification of the spirit). So the mainspring we have been looking for to explain the higher development of forms is the upward-striving consciousness, the "within" of cosmic matter with which we have been dealing. Admittedly the struggle for survival and natural selection also play a part, but the development of life, which clearly strives after increasingly complex forms, can only be explained by this inner movement. Of course, mutations, the sudden changes of hereditary factors, do appear by chance. But the "within" recognizes and takes possession of the advantageous ones among them. That is how development occurs.

To be precise and somewhat simpler:

Up to now, the general opinion has been that a beast of prey developed his predatory instincts because his incisors grew sharp and his feet grew claws. Teilhard de Chardin sees it in reverse. The tiger lengthened his fangs and sharpened his claws because the "within" of his cosmic matter had developed his psyche into the spirit of a beast of prey. A similar process must be assumed to have taken place with the aquatic and rooting animals, birds etc. which, in the course of millions of years, have conquered new realms of life through adaptation. As Teilhard somewhat bluntly expresses it, the living world consists intrinsically of "consciousness" clothed in flesh. All evolution, especially that of life, is the result of a gigantic ramification of the spirit. In other words, the axis on which evolution drives ahead is of a spiritual not a material nature.

IV   The Appearance of Man

Let us now concentrate on the epoch which is decisive for the origin of man. At the end of the Tertiary period the earth was very peaceful. Luxurious forest tracts covered it from South Africa to South America, in Europe and in Asia. These boundless green forests sheltered myriads of antelopes, zebras, many kinds of proboscidians, deer, tigers, wolves and badgers exactly like those of the present day. The only thing missing was smoke rising to the sky from somewhere in the forest. But evolution was not complete. Somewhere, something was accumulating that had to make one last upward step, for the "within" of cosmic matter wanted to explode into a new form. The psychic tension increased. The temperature of consciousness had risen most in the insects and mammals, but the insects had taken wrong directions. For reasons we cannot go into here, their psyche had hardened and become mechanized. They found themselves in a blind alley from which they could not escape. But the instinct of the mammals was not so canalized. It groped onward. The mammals were not one slavish element of the tree like the insects, they were surrounded by a prophetic aura of freedom, almost an aura of personality. For them the horizons of the future were still open. It is among them that the event for which the world was waiting would take place.

But even among the mammals many types found

themselves in morphologic straits. Their vitality had concentrated too much on certain parts of the body, making further development impossible. Many had become slaves of their own means of progress or their armament. Stags, for example, with whole forests of antlers, antelopes with spiral lyres on their foreheads, proboscidians with their gigantic tusks and so on. But the so-called primates, the brain and hand creatures, maintained a conservative attitude. In contrast to the beasts of prey and the proboscidians, they did not develop their teeth any further. In contrast to the ungulates they carefully preserved their five fingers. In fact as far as their members were concerned they remained simple and therefore freer for development of the "within."

The forward urge of evolution neglected everything else in their case and worked only on the brain. Their development disregarded non-essentials. It kept close to the axis on which the development of life works: refinement of the nervous system, perfection of the brain, increase of the "conscious." The "ambition" of this conglomeration was an optimum ambition which is why it met with that success that the whole biosphere had been striving for since the beginning.

All at once, about a million years ago, the most fateful moment for our planet arrived. The great step was taken, an immeasurable step, a step not only onto a new level but into a new order. Like an arrow, man shot out of the conglomeration of hand and brain creatures. He was suddenly there. Silently he appeared, the most mysterious, disrupting being in the cosmos, for whose completely different nature the traditional rules of life could find no place. Externally he could hardly be distinguished from his predecessors. Physically he made his appearance like every other species, a new bud on the tree of life. But internally there had been a revolution, a convulsion of the entire biosphere on a planetary scale. It was he who turned the biosphere of the world into the new order of the noosphere. He made fire, he fashioned stones to fight with, he buried his dead. True, the animals also possessed knowledge, But he did not only look *around* himself, he looked *into* himself! He was the only one who knew he had knowledge. In him the "conscious" of the cosmos saw itself reflected in a mirror for the first time. He had compounded himself, made himself an independent and individual soul. The psychic in man was no longer a mere aureole of the physical. The spirit was now an individual, the indivisible core and focus of the phenomenon. Man was *somebody, a personality*.

This new being would be a paradox if we continued to look at the exterior of evolution only. But as the utterly different physical-spiritual phenomenon, it is living proof that up to now science has neglected a whole dimension of evolution – the "within" of things. Man is the last, palpable piece of evidence that the development of life is only movement of the conscious veiled by morphology.

So we find that at the end of the Tertiary period the psychic temperature in the tree of life had been rising for many hundreds of millions of years. The nervous system had become more and more concentrated and complex. To make this more comprehensible, Pierre Teilhard gives us an illustration: at 99°C. water remains water, at 100°C it boils. The internal equilibrium is completely changed. It enters a new, gaseous aggregation. Similarly "conscious," which had been present in all cosmic matter in greater or less density, concentrated itself more and more until, in man, it crossed the boundary separating the biosphere from the noosphere and was translated into the new order of the self-conscious. Like the origin of life, man's inception was not a gradual process: it was the single, sudden crossing of the borderline between two generations, a kind of mutation into a new nature.

Man was something new. Since he has populated the earth, a dense covering of thinking brains covers our planet, an intellectual envelope, which Teilhard de Chardin calls the "noosphere."

This noosphere is the work of the whole of nature. The *whole* earth has taken part in its creation. It is the result of a total effort on the part of life. Thus humanity is really an arrow that shoots out of the planetary tension of the whole biosphere. That is why man is not just a new branch of the tree of life. Nor is he only a sort of accidental addition which, like some kinds of animals, could die out. Man is the peak toward which all biological efforts on this earth have been aiming, and without which the biosphere would have remained a headless body, a mere torso. Man is the flower of evolution, aspired to from the first, and slowly and methodically prepared for billions of years.

This picture of the earth at the end of the Tertiary period, vast forests filled with myriads of antelopes, zebras, proboscidians, deer, tigers, wolves, foxes, badgers, all hunting each other and eating each other: what a nonsensical state of affairs and what an absurd world!

Only now he is there, the first, the unique being, who looks up to Heaven and comprehends everything. It is he alone who gives meaning to the earlier stages of evolution.

It is clear now that man is not only the last phase of creation, but equally the *inner* reason why all previous development *had* to happen. The rest of creation was only preparation for his habitation, making possible his existence. Man alone gives significance to every stone, every plant, every animal, indeed to the whole universe.

Despite the immeasurable spiritual advance in intelligence, life continued to expand as if nothing had happened. Propagation, dissemination and ramification took their habitual courses *behind* and in front of the threshold of thought. From pre-human times the new being had retained: sexual instinct, the law of propagation, the instinct to fight for life, the curiosity to see and to find out, the urge to hunt and kill for food. All this has survived in us and stems from the unfathomed depths of the biosphere. But everything is transformed by command of the thinking intellect and becomes human.

With man's arrival, the evolutionary urge in the non-human branches appeared to wane. Further exploration of the biosphere had lost its point. One could almost say: the spirit of cosmic matter felt it had reached its goal, the peak of biological evolution.

V The New Meaning of Creation

Pierre de Chardin firmly refuses to commit himself on the question of point Alpha, that is, the emergence of everything out of nothing. In his opinion, the process of creation is only comprehensible to man in its last phases. But these last phases make it clear enough that creation was not a colossal production of all matter in its final form. God allowed matter to rise progressively from the womb of matter. Pierre Teilhard prefers to illustrate the process as a spiral rising from a broad base and gradually diminishing until it reaches its peak. In Teilhard's view, all physical and spiritual matter was there with the first act of creation. It was still enclosed in a more or less embryonic state. It unfolded itself in the course of billions of years, and various individual forms that had been present in it from the beginning emerged at given times. But perhaps this theory can be formulated more clearly as follows: there is only *one* creative act of God. It has been going on for billions of years, it is still happening and will always continue to happen.

True, in the part of *The Phenomenon of Man* dealing with the origin of man, the scientist says the "spiritual thinker" is free to accept any creative work of "special intervention" on God's part under the "veil of the phenomenon." But this remark originated from the year 1948 when he was in Rome, and — as he wrote to the Abbé Breuil – was "touching up his manuscript" to "fit the demands of the censor."

Actually, the idea that God should have "intervened" anywhere in His own work of creation is completely contrary to Teilhard de Chardin's beliefs. A creation, which is unthinkable without the hand of God in even the minutest phase of its course, needs no intervention. Above all the theory that man's soul was, by a special act of God, introduced into the body of an animal, contradicts Teilhard's basic conception of evolution. According to him the psychic precedes the morphologic in the whole of evolution. Evolution is first and foremost the development of the psychic with increasing somatic complexity coming as a result later. The human *soul* makes a body a *human* body.

Anyone, trying to reconcile Teilhard de Chardin's philosophy with former Christian concepts by postulating a special intervention by God in His own work, returns to the theory of a static world. In addition, to speak of "intervention" would entail, logically, the theory that the other stages of evolution had taken place without the constant creative influence of God.

We must be quite clear about this: whoever postulates an "intervention" on the part of God in His own work does not just modify de Chardin's concepts, he destroys the very core of his philosophy. To speak of "the introduction of the human soul through a special act of creation" is to remove all meaning from de Chardin's theory of purposeful evolution of the biosphere toward man. Also his theory of the evolution of the noosphere which, as we shall see, becomes completely unintelligible if one accepts the idea of intervention. We have to accept Teilhard's view of an upward-developing creation up to and including man or reject his entire philosophy.

We have brought these lines of Teilhard de Chardin's thought into clear relief because, at first glance, they seem directly opposed to the official views of the Church. Pope Pius XII's encyclical *Humani generis* of August 12, 1950 suggests to scientists they should explore "the origin of the human body from other living matter already in existence," but adds that the Catholic Faith demands we should believe in "the direct creation of the soul by God." Exhaustive theological inquiries will now have to decide whether Teilhard's opinion, outlined above, that God had created the human soul by gradual degrees, can be reconciled with the Church's teaching. At the same time we should remember that, even according to Teilhard, God is, without any doubt whatsoever, the first cause of every single development in the cosmos. In his concept God's influence is just as necessary and universal as in the static theory of creation. Indeed his view of the creation of man may appear nobler, more in keeping with the other indirect works of God and more worthy of a truly divine way of planning things.

SPECIAL PROBLEMS

The question of "our first parents" is, according to Teilhard de Chardin, an idle one from the scientific point of view. The first traces of man are found at a time when he already populated the world from the

Cape of Good Hope to Peking. The earth's crust shows either no traces of man or shows him later complete and numerous. Here the law is in operation that we mentioned earlier, that nature erases all starting points. She only keeps what is complete and numerous in her archives. As to the question of monogeny (common descent from *one* pair) science gives no answer.

Many anthropologists assume the simultaneous appearance of a whole number of humans along a subtropical zone of the earth. Because the biological tension reached the necessary height in a number of places at the same time, the step into reflective thought resulted, in the same way as mushrooms spring out of the earth at the same moment in different places with the same climatic conditions. Against this opinion Pierre Teilhard is inclined to think that man originated from a single phylum among all the hominidae (monophylism).

The Future of Man

"The world is only interesting when one looks forward" was a favorite saying of Teilhard de Chardin. What will become of man? Where is he going? The scientist repeats over and over again in his letters that this is the only question that ever really interested him. He had spent a lifetime penetrating millions of years into the Palaeozoic era, tracing the line of evolution up to now in order to reach the starting point of the line of man's future development.

His answer to the question: where does man come

from? is unique, but it is in line with the opinions of many other scholars who have studied evolution in the last hundred years. But with the question "What will become of man?" he breaks new ground. The recognition that man emerged like an *arrow* from the biosphere, that he still has a long way to go, that evolution did not finish with the noosphere but has only just been initiated, that man today is only the embryo of what he will eventually become, all this has been brought into discussion in unequivocal terms for the first time by Teilhard de Chardin.

To understand the scientist's theories on this subject correctly, we must first repeat what he meant by the noosphere. In thinking of it we must not picture two or three billion individual brains. True, every man is free to a great extent. But mankind remains as an entity, one branch of the tree of life. In its entirety it remains a biological growth, and its further progress, not only physically but also in relation to the "within," is subject to a great extent to the laws of evolution that have produced it. And therefore this development of mankind remains, without detriment to theology or philosophy, the object of scientific research not only from the somatic, but also from the psychic-spiritual side.

At the same time we must remember that Teilhard's concepts of evolution gave a far wider and more comprehensive picture of it than Darwin's. To the English scientist it was only a transformation of zoological species. According to Teilhard it represented the unalterable interconnection of all existence in the cosmos from the first atom up to mankind. It is the indissoluble chain linking all non-organic matter and all living matter with thinking matter. One cannot omit the smallest molecule of protein or the smallest protozoan without the whole of creation becoming unintelligible.

Further, according to Teilhard, thought was the aim of evolution from the start but evolution does not terminate with the achievement of thought. On the contrary it reaches its peak in man's mind. Only, it is now using methods that have become intellectual. Since *homo sapiens* came into being man's body has hardly altered. Somatically the goal has been reached. But the layer of thinking brains that envelopes the earth continues to evolve, despite the freedom of the individual and according to those laws that have been operative in cosmic matter since the beginning: increase of complexity and increase of consciousness. To put it more drastically: the experiments of our scientists in their laboratories obey the same basic impulses as the experiments of the first cells to achieve higher forms, the only difference being that everything is now on a completely different plane. But once again, as in the previous millions of years, every attempt is being made to achieve improvement. That is the evolution of the noosphere. Man will become still more intensely man. Pierre de Chardin calls this upward progression "hominization."

Without this interpretation of evolution not only natural science, chemistry and physics become unintelligible, but also biology, sociology and the cultural history of mankind.

In de Chardin's opinion, man has been in existence for about a million years. "We" of the twentieth century are the first generation to have had such a clear view of the past as to be able to realize to some extent the immensely long way we have come. We are the first to realize that cosmogenesis and biogenesis have now played their part in this development, but that noogenesis, the evolution of man, is only beginning to enter the picture. The thought that, according to de Chardin, we of today represent an early, still primitive state, is not a very flattering one.

To this is added the realization, continually thrust before us by astronomers, of the minuteness of the place occupied by man in the vastness of the cosmos.

The first reaction of man to all this new knowledge is fear. It is as if the roof and floor of our familiar house had vanished. We had arranged and classified everything so nicely and so permanently and felt ourselves at home. And now we find it was all an illusion! At the thought of the immeasurability of space fear grips us. The Milky Way, in which our sun moves as one of a hundred billion stars on the edge of a convolution covers a space of a hundred thousand light years. But it is only one of an estimated five billion Milky Ways whirling through space. What is man compared to this?

Fear grips us again as we look into time. What are the sixty or seventy years of our life in a cosmos that has existed six or ten billion years? So men feel lost and useless. But according to Teilhard de Chardin this fear is turned to consolation as soon as we realize the reason for evolution. The infinitely great in conjunction with the infinitely small has only one function, to make possible the intermediate stage in which life can build up and in which the cosmos culminates *in* man, not indeed in quantity but in quality. In the same way, the millions of years and the billions of organisms which have preceded us can give cause for comfort when we know that this vast display was necessary in order that the great miracle, man, might emerge from it like an arrow and pursue his own mental path.

But here we come to another question. What if man destroys himself through unbiological behavior, sterilization, total warfare, etc. before the end of his natural biological term of existence, which experts judge to be one or two million years? There are paleontologists who believe that if the human branch vanished from the tree of life, the cosmos would put out another shoot. Another branch of life would enter the mental environment, as when the topmost shoot is cut off a young fir tree another side branch takes over the upward growth.

Teilhard de Chardin does not share this opinion. According to him, evolution on our planet cannot be repeated. Just as the step from albumen amalgamations to the first cell only took place once, so the step into thought is unique and irreversible. As the peak of biogenesis, man is irreplaceable. But for our scientist, a premature destruction of mankind before the completion of his biological term is unthinkable, for man is not only the flower of the tree of life, he is the summit of the universe. The whole of cosmogenesis and biogenesis have no meaning without man. Therefore man *must* reach his goal. If man were prematurely destroyed, the whole universe would founder through the loss of its meaning. And this, according to Teilhard de Chardin, would be absurd. If the world has survived countless unimaginable dangers in the course of billions of years in order to produce humans, it will, despite threats, bring its work to a conclusion by the same methods.

If we want to try and picture the direction in which man is going to progress, we must produce the line of his past evolution into the future to the point of intersection. For this we must bear in mind the providential role played in the past development of man by the rounded shape of the earth. Had the world spread out in an unending flat expanse, man would have spread in all directions. Compression would have played no part. Something that we cannot imagine would have evolved from man, or perhaps nothing at all. But the spherical form forced the twigs of the human branch to bend, to meet each other, to grow over each other, and to form a thick, homogeneous fabric.

Since the later Stone Age, the human race populating the globe has continually been colliding, overlaying and penetrating each other and forming a thick tapestry of human substance. Man is the only organism which has succeeded in forming one single society around the world. That is why the human group is the only one not to have split up into different types but, through inter-breeding, has remained a single, undivided leaf on the tree of life.

This tendency to interweave and strengthen the human fabric is seen particularly clearly in historical times. The Stone Age man still lived on his plot of land. In those days there were humans but no humanity. Included in the life of modern man, however, there are iron, copper, cotton, electricity, films and newspapers. Today to some extent everyone needs the whole earth and the whole of humanity for his life. An isolated man does not think or progress further. The individual can only await the future in the company of everybody else.

Up to now humanity was torn into races and tribes. Their thoughts and wishes were divided. But during the last few decades the human fabric has increased enormously in density. The approach of races and individuals has been completed through railways, cars, airplanes, radio and television. Everyone can influence everyone else. Everyone can be present, actively and passively, on every continent and ocean. This leads to an *enormous concentration of collective human consciousness*. Thus the "planetization" of humanity is being stupendously accelerated today.

Humanity is beginning to think more and more as humanity and to make decisions as humanity. For instance, every single nation on our planet was represented at the opening of the Geophysical Year in 1954. That must have been the first decision to have been made by humanity as a whole. Pierre Teilhard was triumphant. He called 1954 the Year One of the Noosphere.

But all these events are only the outward manifestation of the inward tendency that directs the future evolution of mankind. And it is the "within" above all with which Teilhard de Chardin was concerned.

VI   Point Omega

Teilhard de Chardin tells us that since time began, even in inorganic matter, evolution has been, an increase of the "conscious." It will always remain an increase of the "conscious." Therefore evolution must culminate in some highest degree of the "conscious." Since this "conscious" has risen to the self-conscious in man, to personalization, man's future course must follow the same line, not toward the impersonal, but toward a super-personal. Man's future is obviously a higher centralization of his spiritual substance around one point. Teilhard de Chardin calls this evolutionary goal which is not easy for us to imagine, Point Omega.

It is the end of man's ascent, the cosmic focal point toward which all humanity's mental energies are directed. The attraction causing this centripetal movement is *Love*. Point Omega must then be the cause of this centripetal movement. Therefore Omega is not only a point of future intersection, but must also be already there. Omega, as a super-personal "ego" in the depths of the thinking mass, plays the part of the uniting force. In the same way as the "within" or the "conscious" of cosmic matter was the driving force of evolution, so this Point Omega draws the conscious parts toward itself. Thus Omega is both the axis of development and the goal. Noogenesis mounts irreversibly toward it. Teilhard believes that mankind will need one to two million long, difficult years of war and mental, political and social struggle before reaching this pole – the complete harmony of a united humanity. We have no clear idea as yet of the vast development the noosphere will have to achieve to reach this point, for it is in the nature of evolution that we, an early stage of it, *cannot* picture its further progress. But we must not think only of the individual in this connection.

Even if no great intellects like Plato, Augustine, Thomas Aquinas, Leonardo da Vinci or Goethe were born, we must think of the enormous cumulative and collective forward pressure exercised on the noosphere by the fabric of three billion brains ever more closely in communication with each other. This pressure is toward an increase, an increase in research and knowledge, a closer alliance and increase in love.

THE DIRECTIONS OF HUMAN DEVELOPMENT

Pierre de Chardin sees three directions in the human advance toward the theoretical Point Omega.

First, the increasing improvement in the organization of scientific research. The effects of man's latest discoveries on the universe have been colossal. Mankind will continue to advance along these lines. An increasing number of the mighty forces at present being used for production and armaments will be used by scholars and laboratories in the search for truth. Also the forces continually being freed by machines will be put increasingly at the disposal of science. Everything must be explored and attempted. Man gradually will sublimate his urge to possess into the urge to *know*.

Man will know more in order to understand more, understand more in order to do more, do more in order to be more.

Through the discoveries of nuclear research he has already taken over command of the elements. Through the perfecting of synthetic protein he may one day be able to produce a living organism. In any case he will gain ever greater power over the processes of life through virus research and more exact knowledge of the functions of heredity. Finally, he will gain increasing control of the psychic life. In this way man will increase his influence on the world's course. From the evolutionary viewpoint those who pursue these lines most courageously are the most human of the human race, because they work directly on the axis of human development. Of course this urge to experiment, to discover, to know, is not under man's control! Like the first tentative experiment toward life, it is subject to the evolutionary imperative. Man can do nothing else. He has to make dangerous discoveries as well.

The second line of approach toward Point Omega is toward *mankind* itself. Man has existed for about a million years, but only for the last hundred has he looked back, known who he is and where he comes from. The future will be increasingly an age of the *Science of Man*: because, since man is the goal of evolution, as the subject of research he is the key to the whole universe. So man is really the answer to all our questions. To understand man is to understand how the world came into being and how it will continue to develop. This increase in self-discovery and self-experience will augment and refine the *humane* in man to such an extent that he will use the dangerous weapon of his increasing mastery of the elements less and less against himself.

The third line of approach to Point Omega is the *alliance of science and religion.* For centuries there has been tension between them. According to the Marxists, religion is a phenomenon of the childhood of mankind which will vanish with the progress of social development. Religion used to expound life to man and offer him refuge in need. Now it has been replaced in both roles by science, for science will make the world more and more comprehensible and will be more and more able to master the evils that threaten humanity. As science progresses religion will vanish. That is the Marxist teaching.

Teilhard has other views. After three centuries of struggle neither religion nor science has succeeded in ousting the other. On the contrary, the more clearly modern research illuminates the structure of creation, the more numerous, puzzling and complicated are the metaphysical questions relating to the other side of the cosmos. Obviously science cannot provide the last, all-embracing interpretation of the world. Besides, scientific research itself *can* only continue certain conditions of Faith. For instance, that there is a reason for the universe, that it forms an entity, that it has been created to develop, and so on. According to Teilhard de Chardin, science and religion are not opposites, but only two sides or two phases of a *single,* perfect act of knowledge. Up till now these two sides of knowledge still appear to contradict each other. The nearer mankind approaches Point Omega in the course of thousands and hundreds of thousands of years, the nearer they will approach each other, for the more fully man realizes his place in the universe, the deeper and more intense will be his worship of the Creator. For Teilhard the study of the cosmos and the worship of what he sees as Point Alpha and Omega are already nearly one and the same. He insists: "The more man becomes man, the more necessary will it be for him to worship and to deepen his religion."

CHRIST IN RELATION TO THE WORLD

Finally Teilhard de Chardin turns to the phenomenon of Christ. He emphasizes that his thoughts are not of a scientist but of a Christian, which only Christians will be able to follow in their entirety. Father Teilhard's deliberations can be summarized as follows.

Omega is the active center of attraction around which the evolution of the noosphere is increasingly concentrating. At the same time, it is the goal on which the noosphere is converging. But scientifically this Omega remains an unknown quantity that cannot be more precisely calculated.

This is where the Christian concept comes in. The Christian sees the aim and evolution of the universe as follows: Creation came from God, from Point Alpha. It culminated, qualitatively, in man and perfects itself through the return of thinking beings to God. God-made-Man is in this last phase of return, in other words, Omega. As God-made-Man Christ is simultaneously the axis and final goal of salvation. He is the transcendent pole toward which all souls are striving. He is the highest Being, toward whom the progressive personalization of mankind aims. Christ is the center of strength, already there, already operating, attracting, purifying, inspiring through love: drawing the whole noosphere together, transforming it and leading it back to the divine center. Christ, God-made-Man as the Evangelists and St. Paul proclaim Him, can therefore fulfill, in the highest degree, the function of Point Omega. But whether Christ is really the Point Omega, postulated for the future development of mankind, cannot be scientifically proved. To confirm it is a matter of Faith and Christian teaching. Teilhard de Chardin himself considers this coincidence of Omega with Christ to be self-evident. In his opinion this is the point where the two sides must converge and reach full agreement about the meaning of the universe.

According to him, the birth of the Son of God in the night at Bethlehem is no longer an isolated event in cosmic history, no longer a more or less extraneous irruption of the supernatural into the world. The Incarnation of Christ is the consummation of the world, its last ascent to a reality incomprehensible until it happened. In the historical person of Jesus of Nazareth, Point Omega appears tangibly for the first time. With Christ's Incarnation another step into a new order was taken, whereby the axis of the noosphere's development coincided with the "axis of God."

This last phase had been foreseen from the beginning. Indeed it was the true reason for the creation of man, just as man was the true reason for the evolution of the cosmos. It would be just as impossible therefore to dispense with the Incarnation without destroying the whole meaning of the cosmos, as it would be to dispense with the birth of the first cell or of reflective thought. Seen from the cosmic point of view, the Incarnation is not a paradox. For millions of years nature had been preparing for the reception of grace. God *had* to become man in order to reincorporate in Himself the peak of evolution. Thus the goal of the cosmos and the goal of salvation are identical. From cosmogenesis came biogenesis, from biogenesis, noogenesis, and finally from noogenesis came Christogenesis, the crowning aim of all, as John and Paul saw it.

From the cosmic viewpoint, what Father Teilhard tries to do is to take the Christ-figure out of the incredibly narrow historical frame into which it had been forced, and project it onto the universe, where Christ would become the focal point and the *true perfector of evolution.* He is the Lord of the cosmos. *Omnia per ipsum facta sunt, et sine ipso factum est nihil.*

According to this, to follow Christ is not a flight from the world, but submission to the world. Worship does not mean putting God before all things, but seeking God in and through all things, giving oneself with heart and soul to the act of creation which is taking place all the time, associating oneself with it and thus, through work and research which, rightly viewed, is worship, to bring the world to final perfection in Point Omega.

Teilhard de Chardin's views on Christianity can be summed up as follows.

Nearly all current religions are so closely linked up with mythological fantasy and so much in the grip of passivity and world pessimism that the new scientific-evolutionary discoveries will present them with a crisis which they will not be able to survive. It also seems clear to him that the gospel of Christianity has been severely shaken during the last three hundred years and will be still more shaken today. But he considers the Christian Faith to be sufficiently vital, flexible, bold and progressive to continue to raise the question of the "unknown God" and not only to assimilate the new concepts of the world but even to gain an undreamed of impetus from them.

In actual fact the evolutionary view of the world provides wonderful new and wider possibilities of recognizing and drawing nearer to God. According to Teilhard we are going to leave the age of *religions* and enter the age of *Religion*. The ecumenical movement within Christianity points in this direction. The intellect and spirit have expanded most in Christianity. Of all religions it most closely follows the lines pursued by anthropogenesis. Thus, evolution will continue along the axis of a self-evolving Christianity. On this axis other world religions will converge. The goal of this evolution is Omega, Christ the Almighty, the haven and refuge of mankind. According to St. Paul, He is the Savior who continues to exist in His Mystical Body in mankind, the soul of this universal union. Through this we may glimpse the dynamic part that the Church of the future will play in the evolution of mankind.

The *problem of Christian faith* is also a problem of evolution in Pierre Teilhard's opinion. The present phase of evolution is the reason for the faith's apparent lack of clarity and God's seemingly blurred image. In our present state we are not capable of seeing more clearly God's diaphaneity, the effulgence of God's glory penetrating through this world. True, God does not conceal Himself, that would be impossible for a righteous God. It is only because of our present imperfection that God *cannot* show Himself to us clearly enough as yet. He watches over His creation as a mother watches over her newborn child. But its eyes are still blind, and it is incapable of recognizing its origin. It will grow toward this origin from day to day with increasing consciousness.

We only want to mention briefly here that Teilhard de Chardin also considered the problem of man's *continued existence after death* as seen from the evolutionary viewpoint. Thinking man has evolved through millions of years of creative process from inorganic matter. It would be absurd to think he could sink back into inorganic matter through total death. Absolute death would destroy the meaning of evolution. Since the world's very existence has proved a hundred times over to be a reasoned process, this process could not come to a senseless end in absolute death. Since the cosmos is striving after more and more consciousness and more and more unity, the idea that mankind, its apotheosis, should disintegrate is false logic, measuring spiritual values by material standards.

60

As soon as the universe admitted thought, it could be no longer transitory. By its very nature it must emerge into the absolute. The spirit will always succeed, as it always has succeeded, in mastering dangers and difficulties. It represents the indestructible side of the universe.

VII   The Discussion Raised by Teilhard's Concepts

In the foregoing pages we have tried to give a rough outline, although with some perhaps unsatisfactory abridgements and simplifications, of Teilhard de Chardin's theories of the world and mankind, insofar as this is possible on the basis of the writings published to date. Final judgment cannot be passed on his interpretation of the cosmos until all his works have been published and the ensuing discussions among the experts have produced definite results. All we want to do here is to append a few remarks that may tempt the reader to study the works himself.

About one hundred and twenty articles by Teilhard on zoology, geology and paleontology appeared during his lifetime in various scientific periodicals in Europe, America and the Far East, and about ninety essays of a philosophical and religious nature. But his chief works. *Le Phénoméne Humain, L'Apparition de l' Homme, La Vision du Passé, Le Milieu Divin, L'Avenir de l'Homme, Le Groupe Zoologique Humain,* remained unpublished until his death in 1955. They have been brought out since by a committee composed of scholars from all parts of the world. As we have said, the editions have already run into numbers quite unprecedented for literature of this kind. Today, Teilhard's theories are the theme of lectures, radio talks, newspaper articles and books in philosophical circles all over the world.

It is only this interpretation of mankind that comes as a real relief to all those eager students of modern scientific progress, who up to now had searched in vain for a satisfactory religious interpretation of the present day concept of the world. To these people Teilhard de Chardin brings incalculable consolation. In these circumstances, it is understandable if enthusiasm gets a little exuberant and leads to occasional exaggeration.

That enthusiasm can easily become the enemy of reason is well known. Teilhard would be the first to smile at this and to check any exaggerated veneration. Not only his innate modesty would make him do so but, still more, the fact that he, as a student of evolution, knew only too well that it is doubtful whether man will ever possess the final key to wisdom. Such a colossal synthetic experiment *cannot* succeed at the first attempt. That would contradict all the experience of past learning. The first appearance of a truth has always been accompanied by errors. The decisive feature is the leaven that causes ferment and thereby eventual clarification.

Teilhard himself always opposed the unquestioning acceptance of the theories of an Aristotle, an Augustine or a Thomas Aquinas. These unique figures appeared to him almost as mutations in the history of man's intellect which evolution may have outdated, but without which present philosophy would be unthinkable. Referring to this subject he said of himself: "I have only one great wish, to find myself projected into the center of new developments."

To appreciate his unique place in the science of

physical anthropology we must bear in mind that many of the ideas of his magnificent vision of the evolutionary process had long been prevalent when he incorporated them brilliantly into his work. None of the greatest ones are completely original. For instance, the theory of interiority's being the driving force of evolution, the idea of a noosphere with its own laws, the discovery of the converging tendencies of the progress of mankind, were subjects of discussion in some cases *before* Teilhard and in some independently of him. But Teilhard's activities in the laboratory, his continuous hard work, his unceasing journeys to all parts of the world and permanent contact with the research work of his fellow scientists, enabled him to use contemporary knowledge and to transform it into one great concept.

EVIL IN THE WORLD

Naturally, as Teilhard expected, serious doubts were cast on his theories. For one thing his ideas were held by some to be too optimistic. Evil, misery and sin which play so large a part in the literature and daily life of man had no place in his concept. Teilhard replied personally to this criticism and declared that, for the sake of clarity, he had only wanted to show the *positive* side of evolution, the negative side would then become obvious. In actual fact evolution consists of one success out of millions of attempts. Very little in the world progresses, an incalculable mass goes wrong, is unfit to survive and founders. This means sorrow enough in the biosphere! In the noosphere loneliness and fear are added. Man's tentative intellectual experiments to find what the universe is and what it holds for him bring him untold worry and despondency. The ever-increasing conjuncture of cultures is bound to lead to disagreements and strife. Therefore, evolution is at the same time man's destiny and his problem.

Even the convergence on Point Omega will be accompanied by mistakes and failures, because harmony will always be disrupted by irrational behavior. So not even this last ascent will be accomplished without a multitude of errors and sins.

Nevertheless the scientist considers that, in a static cosmos, where creation emerged suddenly and complete from the hands of the Creator, evil would be completely inexplicable. How could evil come from the hand of an almighty and all-bountiful God? Is that not the problem on which theologians have been laboring for centuries? But if we see the universe as being in a state of becoming, imperfections must obviously be a part of the process, since anything arranging itself must necessarily include some disorder at every stage. Thus evil is structural stress of evolutionary creation. It counts for nothing in itself. In the biosphere it is only a principle of propulsion and in the noosphere a factor of spiritualization.

And Pierre Teilhard cannot regard death as evil. He has no sympathy with the existentialist's deprecation of the world and apocalyptic lamentations, or for the "Sein zum Tode" of Heidegger. The whole literature of lamentation was a foreign language for him. For him death is a necessity for the ascent of life. The individual has to be removed from the earth's surface and replaced by another, otherwise the spiral cannot rise. And that it does rise is alone decisive.

The second half of his most important theological work, *Le Milieu Divin,* is devoted exclusively to the *Divinisation des Passivités.* In it human suffering in every form, especially sickness and death, is given a religious interpretation for which it is difficult to find an equal in depth and width of vision.

THEOLOGICAL DOUBTS

Theologians, however, have other misgivings that are more difficult to answer. They find that Point Alpha, the God of Creation, is not shown clearly enough in Teilhard's concept of the world. They also profess to find in his universal view of matter, life and thought, that he attributes a sort of common soul to everything, and that the human soul is distinguished from it only in degree and not in nature. Man is not, therefore, visible in his entire greatness, above all not in his unique, transcendental, self-surpassing place in God's scheme of salvation.

The theologians also have difficulty in reconciling the biblical teaching on Paradise, the Fall, and Original Sin, with the new theories. To this is added the fear that the triumphant vision of Christ the "Cosmocrat," the perfector of evolution, leaves no place for Redemption and the Cross. Finally the biblical epiphany of the Son is nearly eclipsed by the diaphaneity of God in the world.

Somewhat summarily abridged, these are the chief misgivings expressed by theologians, and they cannot be lightly dismissed by any Christian. In such vitally important questions, conscience demands the most meticulous examination. On the other hand, we can reasonably expect that theological science should not lightly dismiss the new theory of mankind presented by Teilhard de Chardin, nor the wealth of factual evidence on which he bases it. No purpose is served by labeling Teilhard's grandiose world concept "Monism," "Pantheism," "Panpsychism" or any other handy "ism" in order to dispose of it more easily. In this connection one has only to think what unfortunate results a similar attitude toward Galileo or Darwin had for Christianity. The Church cannot allow herself this sort of thing at a time when such powerful scientific forces are at work all over the world to discover the nature and meaning of the cosmos.

The intellectual achievement of Teilhard de Chardin not only causes admiration; it also demands respect and caution on the part of anyone preparing to pass judgment on his account of creation. Only the most delicate instruments can be used here to extract the timeless truth: clumsy ones are too liable to extract an error.

VIII   The Significance of
Pierre Teilhard de Chardin

Teilhard de Chardin broke through the No-man's-land separating science and theology. He offered for discussion a fascinating theory for a solution to the problem of evolution. It rests on a sympathetic understanding of the world which, at the moment, is as much a vital necessity for Christianity as it is for scientific research. Teilhard de Chardin envisions man not only somatically but also in mind and soul, as representative of the advancement on the pre-anthropoid stages demanded by evolution. He thereby leads man upward from his biological genesis to the point where, without a break in the chain of events, theology can take him over as the object of the supernatural scheme of redemption. By stressing the spiritual perspective of evolution and showing how the gropings of millions of years were aimed at spiritual consummation in the formation of personality, he tried to give a really convincing and constructive answer to materialistic atheism. By his active, energetic attitude toward the realities of the world as they are recognized and understood today, he declared war on the ignorance, apathy, pessimism and passivity too often displayed by Christians, and brought them once more to the forefront in all spheres where, through technical control of the universe and inductive metaphysics, science is still searching for the meaning of creation and mankind.

It is easy to understand what an exciting task it must be for a professional theologian to immerse himself in Teilhard's work, to examine carefully the whole evidence, to pay the same serious attention to paleontological conclusions as to theology, and to demonstrate courageously to us what part of the Catholic Church's teaching up to now on the origin of man is really theology, what part is made up of outdated philosophical concepts or the clothing of theological statements in the language of their time. This work is certainly not easy, but it cannot be avoided, for it is a pastoral duty in the highest sense of the term.

Above all, priests, teachers and all who help to form the minds of present-day youth, will have to study the import of Teilhard de Chardin's philosophy. Any evasion of this vital question in the future would be shirking responsibility. Those, too, whose chief joy it is to follow closely in the steps of the pioneers of cosmology, must *enter into* his philosophy. This does not mean they need shut themselves up in it.

In this connection another question arises. During the last few years various suggestions have been put forward on how to remedy the prevailing shortage of priests. The opinion has often been expressed that the clergy who deal with the sciences and who instruct the young in these subjects have wandered drastically from their priestly vocations. It has been suggested that priests working on profane sciences should be recalled and employed in "practical parish duties."

During this same period Father Teilhard thought of

another plan. Shortly before his death he suggested that the Church should select the best scientific minds among secular and regular priests and put them at the disposal of laboratories, scientific expeditions and universities all over the world. In his opinion, wherever a priest is working to increase the diaphaneity of God in the world, he is fulfilling a pastoral duty.

Teilhard de Chardin was convinced that the reconciliation of Church and science and the integration, so vitally necessary, of a modern cosmic-Christian philosophy could only take place if a great working society of theologians existed who would study the phenomenon of man's origins, not only among dogmatists but also in daily contact with the research going on continually in the world.

Another suggestion must not be forgotten here: experts on the intellectual development of communism are always pointing out that its appeal to youth lies above all in the forward-looking ideology with its belief in the future, in the belief that through technology and science the man of the future will gain increasing dominion over himself and the world. Teilhard de Chardin also said, "Marxists *believe* in the future of mankind while present-day Christians do not."

In this connection we must be quite clear how exclusively retrospective our theological philosophy is. Of course it is in the nature of Christian revealed religion that we should see the problems of existence retrospectively. We look *back* to the words of the Bible, *back* to the teaching of the early Church, *back* to the opinions of the Fathers of the Church, and *back* to the great theologians of former centuries. And yet it is to be desired that a serious coming to grips with Teilhard's view should lead to new dimensions in our religious philosophy, to a *forward* and an *outward* view.

Pronouncements from seats of learning and pulpits must do greater justice to the perspectives in which the increasingly cosmic and technically-minded human race thinks. The Church must interpret theologically not the world of yesterday, but the world of today and to-morrow. Religion has at no time been merely a means of personal salvation but rather it is always an interpretation of the world as well.

THE PERSONALITY OF TEILHARD DE CHARDIN

Father Pierre Teilhard de Chardin whose inspired and aristocratic character seems, in the greatness and purity of his mind, to be an anticipation of that "hominization" which he expected of the future, is described as tall and thin, the latter the result of ceaseless travel. His fine but energetic features were marked by the winds of sea and desert. Warm, brown eyes glinted, kindly but critical, beneath a high forehead. Around his mouth were innumerable little ironical lines. The long-fingered scientist's hands were mobile, and even as he grew older his whole bearing remained youthful.

Teilhard de Chardin was a man of dialogue. Wherever he appeared he radiated optimism and confidence. Everyone was struck by his attraction and warmth of character. His need to meet new people and to try his ideas out in conversation with them, was just as unquenchable as the urge to reap the fruits of an active life of endless ocean voyages and weeks of monotonous desert travel, and to give himself up to meditation on the final secrets of life.

Teilhard de Chardin's lot was a hard one. His was the almost unexampled case of a thinker to whom it was not granted to see even one of his major works in print. He is a tragic example of that conflict between personal convictions and discipline that so easily arises when an exceptional brain is too far in advance of the ideas of his times.

There were two ways in which he could have avoided the conflict: to lay aside the habit of his Order or to sacrifice his conscience as a scientist. Despite bitter experience and despite his unshakable faith in the rightness of his philosophy, this "most revolutionary thinker of European Christianity in the twentieth century," as Friedrich Heer calls him, never attempted to loosen the ties binding him to the Society of Jesus or to the Church.

A letter written by him from South Africa in October 1951 to the worried General of the Society in Rome, which his friend Father Leroy published in 1960, is a moving witness to this heroic attitude. There was never one word of complaint in his letters. He was not an ambitious man, in fact his only passion was to speculate, to question and to experiment. He chose silence. The strength to do so was drawn from his unshakable conviction that a thought, properly conceived in any part of the universe, could not be destroyed. He knew that his ideas would be brought to fruition later by others. He died a lonely man. Like Moses on the mountain he saw the promised land, but it was not granted him to lead the people into it.